W9-CNA-980

WE WERE HERE FIRST
THE NATIVE AMERICANS

THE
LENAPE

Michael DeMocker

PURPLE TOAD
PUBLISHING

WE WERE HERE FIRST
THE NATIVE AMERICANS

Copyright © 2016 by Purple Toad Publishing, Inc.   Printing   1   2   3   4   5   6   7   8   9

PUBLISHER'S NOTE: The data in this book has
been researched in depth, and to the best
of our knowledge is factual. Although every
measure is taken to give an accurate account,
Purple Toad Publishing makes no warranty of
the accuracy of the information and is not
liable for damages caused by inaccuracies.

Publisher's Cataloging-in-Publication Data
DeMocker, Michael.
   Lenape / written by Michael DeMocker.
     p. cm.
   Includes bibliographic references and index.
   ISBN 9781624691621
1. Delaware Indians—Juvenile literature. I.
Series: We were here first.
E99.D2 2016
973.04973
                    Library of Congress Control Number:
                                          2015908069

eBook ISBN: 9781624691638

CONTENTS

"The wolf ran as fast as he could through the lush forest."

INTRODUCTION
THE GIANT TURTLE

The wolf ran as fast as he could through the lush forest. His tongue lolled from his mouth as his panting kept pace with the thunder of his paws striking the forest floor. He had been running for days, trying to reach a huge green hill that always seemed just out of reach. He heard the distant howls of his pack behind him, begging him to return, but he was so close… so close…

Suddenly he broke from the woods and into an open field. The green hill was just ahead and he increased his speed, sure he would finally make it. The huge green hill turned and two enormous eyes opened and stared right at the wolf. The hill was the head of a giant turtle. The wolf had been running on its back as the turtle grew larger, creating the world.

With a start, the young Lenape (LEH-nuh-pee) boy woke up from his dream.

"Grandfather, I dreamed I was a wolf last night," the boy told the old man.

"You had a vision, my son," said his grandfather, nodding in approval.

The Lenape believed that long ago the world was swallowed in a great flood because of a fight between a giant toad and a giant snake.

"Do we really live on the back of a giant turtle?" the boy asked.

The old man sighed, looked off into the woods, and retold the story once told to him by his grandfather. Long ago a fight between a giant toad and a giant snake caused a great flood. As the waters rose to cover the mountaintops, the spirit Nanapush, grandfather of animals and men, climbed to the top of a tree.

Nanapush gathered the birds and animals and sang a song to stop the waters from rising. He put the branches of the tree on top of a turtle to make a raft for the animals. Then he thought about how a new world could be made. He spoke with the animals, telling them he needed soil from the earth deep beneath the waves. A beaver volunteered to dive down, but eventually his drowned body came back to the surface. Nanapush breathed life back into it. A diving bird called a loon tried next, but he also came back without the soil.

A puny muskrat then dove in. He was under the water a very long time, and he too came back drowned, but he had some soil on his snout. Nanapush returned him to life and blessed him. The spirit put the soil on the back of the turtle and sang a song. The turtle grew and grew. After a time, Nanapush sent out a bear to find the edge of the turtle. The bear came back a few days later, saying he'd found the edge.

Next, as the turtle continued to grow, Nanapush sent out a deer, which came back weeks later having found the edge. Finally, Nanapush sent out a wolf. The wolf did not return, so Nanapush decided the turtle had grown large enough. On the beautiful new earth, a tree grew, and the tree bent to touch the ground. There grew the first man and the first woman, and this couple filled the new earth with people.

"So yes, grandson, that is why we call this land Turtle Island and why to this day, the wolves howl at night, trying to call home their missing ancestor whom Nanapush sent out to find the edge of the new world."

His grandson sat for a moment, and then smiled. "A simple yes or no would have done, Grandpa, but thanks for the story."

"Just like his father," the old man grumbled.[1]

The spirit Nanapush sent the animals out one by one to find the edge of the giant turtle.

In 1626, Peter Minuit, of the Dutch West India Company, gave a group of Native Americans, believed to be a Lenape tribe called the Canarsee, 60 guilders worth of goods in exchange for use of what is now the island of Manhattan (*manna-hata* in Lenape, meaning "hilly island"). Though the Canarsee got the gift, it was mostly the Wappinger Indians, closely related to the Lenape, who actually lived on the island.

The Dutch thought they were buying Manhattan, but Native Americans did not think people could own land any more than a person could own the water or sky. They thought they were getting a gift simply for sharing the land.

CHAPTER 1
LIFE IN LENAPEHOKING

The Native American tribe called the Lenni-Lenape, or just Lenape, lived in the Delaware Valley on the east coast of North America. The Lenape called their homeland *Lenapehoking*, meaning "Land of the Lenape." Their territory included parts of the modern states of Pennsylvania, New Jersey, Delaware, and Maryland. When the Europeans first came to North America to colonize what they called the New World, the Lenape Indians were some of the first people they met.

The name *Lenape*, pronounced *LEH-nuh-pee* or *leh-NAH-pee*, means "the People." (Lenni-Lenape means "the Real People.") European settlers called these people the Delaware Indians, after the lands where the Lenape lived: Delaware. The settlers had named the land for Englishman Thomas West, the Baron De La Warr, who was governor of Virginia.

Whether it is true or not, there is a humorous story about how the tribe came to accept being called the Delaware. It is said when a newly arrived European asked a Lenape what tribe he belonged to, the visitor could not pronounce the name he was told: Lenape. After several tries, he got it right. The native exclaimed in his own language, *"Nal në ndëluwèn!"** meaning, "That's what I said!" The tongue-tied European heard *dëluwèn*, which sounded like *Delaware*, and the name stuck.[1]

*The Lenape words in this book are pronounced as they are spelled.

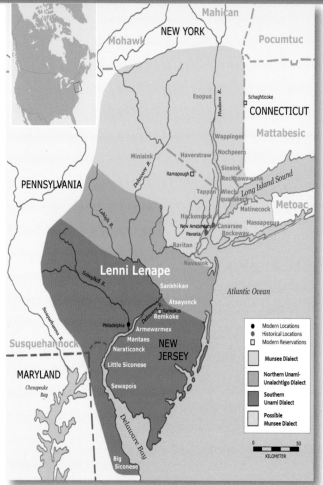

Delaware Indian territories

In the 1600s, about forty Lenape groups lived throughout the Delaware Valley. The groups shared a language, tribal marriages, and strategic alliances. Neighboring tribes called the Lenape "the Grandfathers" out of respect for their ability to negotiate peace between neighboring tribes. According to stories handed down through the generations, the Lenape homeland was also the birthplace of all the Algonquin tribes.

These forty groups belonged to three larger groups. Each one spoke a dialect of the Eastern Algonquian language. The Munsee, or People of the Stony Country, lived north of the Raritan River. (The Raritan River runs through what is now central New Jersey.) The Unami, or People Down River, lived south of the Raritan. A third group—the Unalactigo, or People by the Ocean—were blended into the Unami by the late 1600s.[2]

A sachem, or chief, chosen for his wisdom and fairness, led each village. In times of war, the tribe would select a war chief, a warrior skilled in battle and tactics. In a Lenape village, everything was shared, including the work—and there was a great deal of work. In order to eat, the Lenape grew crops, hunted, trapped, and fished.

Men were in charge of building houses, making tools, clearing the land for farming, and crafting canoes. If their village needed to be defended, the men took the role of warriors.

The men also hunted and trapped animals for food and for their pelts. Whitetail deer, elk, and bears were their main prey, but they also trapped smaller animals, including turkeys, rabbits, and raccoons. The Lenape hunters held nature in great respect. In order to avoid angering the spirits, they observed religious traditions when going on a hunt.

The Lenape were also excellent fishermen. They would place a row of stakes or piles of rocks in a river to make a kind of fence called a fish weir. Using this and fishing nets, the Lenape caught perch, bass, trout, and catfish. They also caught spawning saltwater fish like shad and sturgeon. Turtles, shrimp, oysters, and crabs were caught, too. Once the fish were in the nets, the Lenape would spear them or simply grab them with their bare hands. Then the women gutted, split, and hung the catch to dry in the sun on a wooden rack. Some of the meat would be eaten right away. The rest would be dried for the winter.

A weir stretches across the water to trap fish. The use of weirs dates back to early mankind, and is still used by people around the world.

Along with their fish-gutting duties, the women gathered foods that grew in the wild, such as berries, fruits, and nuts. They also planted and harvested crops. Their three main crops—corn, beans, and squash—were called the Three Sisters. Like the dried meat, some of these plant foods would be put away for the winter.

Lenape women cooked and cleaned the house, sewed and repaired clothing, dried food for storage, kept the fires burning year-round, and looked after the children. Women were respected in Lenape society and were considered equally important as the men within the tribe. Wives were free to make up their own minds, no matter what their husbands thought.

Lenape children learned from the tribe everything they would need to know when they grew up. Boys learned to hunt game by practicing sneaking, how to use weapons, and studying how animals behaved. They also became skilled at woodworking so that they could craft canoes and wooden bowls. Wrestling matches and races taught Lenape boys the skills they would need as warriors.

Girls learned agriculture and sewing, and how to make baskets and pottery. The Lenape were great at making clay pots for cooking. They could make rounded cooking pots large enough to hold two deer at once!

Wolves, Turtles, and Turkeys
The Lenape people were divided into three *phratries* (FRAH-treez), or family groups. Over the years, the names of these phratries became simplified as the Wolf, the Turtle, and the Turkey. Within each phratry, there were about a dozen sub-clans, with names like Dog Standing by the Fire, Snapping Turtle, and Bird Cry. The Lenape phratries were matrilineal, which means they were passed down on the mother's side of the family. If your mother was of the Turkey clan, then you were a Turkey, too. When you grew up, you could not marry a Turkey; you had to marry someone from the Wolf or Turtle clan. Your children would then be in the same clan as their mother.[3]

For twenty years, Big Moon lived with the spirits of thunder, lightning, and rain.

One day, Big Moon disappeared while hunting. He was not seen for twenty years. When he returned, he told the tribe he had been living at the top of the mountains and that his friends were the spirits of thunder, lightning, and rain. The young spirits were mischievous and would cause lightning to strike the world below. They also caused tornadoes and storms, especially when they were angered. The older spirits, he said, were calmer. They brought the rain needed for their crops.

A young woman from the village fell in love with Big Moon, and the elder women sent her to become his wife. Big Moon refused, saying he had married a rain spirit during his years away, and that his spirit wife would be jealous if he were with someone else. The elder women laughed at him, saying his spirit wife was too far away to care. Big Moon agreed to have the young maiden brought to his house.

When his bride-to-be arrived, a violent storm of wind, rain, and lightning struck the village. Big Moon told the girl to hide in his house, and he went into the woods. The storm stopped and he soon returned. To the amazement of the tribe, he was not wet. His intended bride ran back to her home and did not return.

Big Moon grew old with the tribe but remained alone. He went along on the hunts, keeping the rain away or bringing the rain when needed. For the rest of his life, he was called Rainmaker.[4]

Small Lenape families lived in wigwams, small domed homes built with sticks and covered with bark, woven mats, or animal skins.

CHAPTER 2
FOOD, SHELTER, AND TRANSPORTATION

The Lenape lived in villages of various sizes. Larger villages had several hundred people, but most of them had just a few dozen. The Lenape did not live in tepees like the Plains Indians. Instead they lived in wigwams. They bent sticks into the shape of a dome, and then covered the dome with bark, woven mats, or animal skins. Each wigwam would be home to a small family.

Larger, rectangular buildings called longhouses, or barkhouses, were built for several families. The barkhouse was heated with a firepit in the center, where cooking was done. The smoke escaped through holes in the roof, which could be closed when it rained or snowed. Grains and vegetables, such as corn, were hung to dry from racks on the ceiling, and then stored under the beds or on shelves. Food was also stored in the barkhouse inside holes dug from the earth, particularly during the winter when the ground outside was frozen.

Another structure found in the Lenape village was the *pimewakan*, or sweat hut. It served as a place of worship, a medical tent, and a public bath. Built like a wigwam, the sweat hut worked like a sauna. Water was poured over heated rocks,

The *pimewakan,* or sweat hut, served as a place of worship, a medical tent, and a public bath.

and the hut filled with steam. It was believed that illness or bad spirits could be sweated from the body through this ritual.

The Lenape generally did not travel very far from their village, preferring to hunt and farm within a well-chosen area for as long as it could support them.[1] When they needed to go farther, whether for hunting, trading, or ceremonies, the Lenape usually just walked, making use of trails and dry streambeds.

Since native horses died out in North America over 10,000 years before, there were no beasts of burden except for dogs. (The Spanish brought horses back to America in the sixteenth century.) For the most part, the Lenape carried their cargo on their backs. When carrying a heavy burden, such as firewood, women would use a strap called a tumpline. It went across the top of the head so that the spine could help take some of the weight from the shoulders. Men would put the strap across the chest when carrying a hefty load, such as a dead deer.[2]

To make a dugout canoe, the Lenape felled trees, let them dry out for several weeks, and then hollowed them out using fire and sharp stone tools.

After winter gave way to spring and the rivers and lakes were no longer frozen, the Lenape could also travel by canoe. They felled trees, let them dry for several weeks, and then hollowed them out with fire and scraping tools. These "dugout" canoes could be over forty feet long and able to carry dozens of people. Chestnut, oak, and elm trees were mainly used to make the canoes. The tulip tree—or *Muxulhemenshi,* which means "tree which makes the canoe"—was also a good choice.[3]

How did they cut the trees down? What kinds of scraping tools did they use? For the Lenape, nature was their hardware store. They used stones of different sizes and shapes to make arrowheads, axes, knives, hammers, and kitchen utensils. They used hammer stones to shape and whetstones to smooth and sharpen their tools. Sometimes the shaped stones would be tied to a piece of wood, a process called "hafting," to make tools like axes, spears, and mallets.[4]

Hafted arrowhead

17

Lenape Moccasins

The animals they hunted gave the Lenape other tools: turtle shells were used as bowls, and the bones and antlers of elk and deer were fashioned into fishhooks, sewing needles, and even toys. They used the fiber of the deer's tendons to make thread for sewing and strings for their bows. Deer hooves were boiled to make glue.

The Lenape received not just food and tools from the animals they hunted, but also their clothing. They tanned the hides of deer and elk to dress themselves with moccasins, breechcloths, and bandoliers, a kind of purse. These were very helpful, especially since Lenape clothing didn't have pockets.

Women wore skirts made of deerskin. When traveling through heavy, scratchy brush, the Lenape put on deerskin leggings to protect their skin.

Bearskins became warm robes in the cold winters, and turkey feathers were made into toasty cloaks. Fur mittens and hats also helped the Lenape battle the frigid winters, when the spirits of ice and snow could make life unpleasant.

Warm robes were fashioned from bearskins to keep the Lenape warm during the cold winters.

A wooden frame stretched the deerskin so that it could be used to make clothing, moccasins, or bandoliers.

To make the pelts ready to wear, the Lenape first stretched the animal's skin and scraped off all the extra fat (a process called "fleshing") and hair ("beaming"). The deer's brains were then stirred into a mushy paste, and the paste was massaged into the pelt, making it soft. The deerskin was stretched on a wooden frame. Finally, it was rolled into a cone, kind of like a tepee, and smoked over a fire for hours, which made it flexible. After it aired out for a few days, the deerskin was ready to be made into clothing.[5]

A Lenape teenager would go on a vision quest, traveling for days without food or water, hoping to meet the guardian spirit that would guide and protect him or her throughout life.

CHAPTER 3
OF SPIRITS AND GAMES

According to the Lenape, a Great Spirit named Kishelemukong created the universe and everything in it. They believed that Kishelemukong was not overly concerned with the goings-on of man. That job was left to minor spirits called *manetuwak*. These guardian spirits inhabited everything in nature, from animals to trees to the weather. They were respected and honored through rituals and offerings in the places where they lived. Whenever the Lenape cut down a tree or killed an animal, they thanked its *manetu* for the sacrifice.[1]

When a Lenape became a teenager, he or she would be sent on a vision quest to find his or her guardian spirit. The youngster would travel alone into the woods without food or water, sometimes for several days. If the teen was fortunate, the guardian would appear to become the spirit that guided and protected the child throughout life. Once the teen had a vision, there would be a naming ceremony. The teenager would be given his or her permanent name, by which he or she would be known from then on. After the naming ceremony, the teenager would be considered an adult.

The Lenape held a twelve-day annual harvest ceremony in autumn called the *Gamwing,* or Big House Ceremony. The roof of the council house represented the Creator above and the floor was the earth below. A wooden pole connected the earth to the heavens. The walls were the four quarters of the earth created by Kishelemukong. A dozen carved faces of spirit gods were placed around the house. Over the days of the ceremony, visions were recounted, dances performed, and songs were sung to give thanks for the blessings of the year past and to seek good fortune in the year to come.

Many Lenape ceremonies were celebrated through dance, like the Corn Harvest Dance. The autumn Mask Dance was held to bring a fortunate hunting season. The Doll Dance was a springtime event where dancers carried dolls tied to sticks. Drums, rattles, and flutes provided the music for the dancing, which could go long into the night.

Even though there was always a great deal of work to do in Lenape society, the people did find time for fun. They enjoyed many sports and

Many Lenape ceremonies were celebrated through dance, like the Corn Harvest Dance.

Pick-up sticks

games. One of their favorites was *Pahsahëman,* a kind of springtime soccer match pitting males against females. Outsiders first observed and documented the game in the early seventeenth century.

The Lenape played other games as well, like *Selahtikàn,* their version of pick-up sticks. Decorated reeds were mixed with plain ones and dropped onto a blanket. Players would then try to score points by picking up the decorated reeds without upsetting the rest.[2]

If you've ever played the ball-and-cup game, where you try to flip a ball tied to a string into a cup on a handle, you may be good at the Lenape game *Kokolesh,* or "Rabbit Tail." Instead of a ball, this game uses a cone with a rabbit tail on the end . The cone is tied to a sharp stick. The idea was to catch the cone on the end of the stick.

A dice game called *Mamandin* was played for points. The Lenape fashioned dice from bones, antlers, or fruit pits decorated on one side. Five or seven dice were

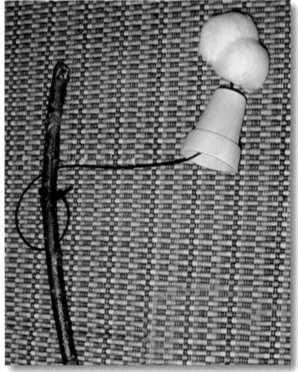

Kokolesh

placed in a wooden bowl and turned over on a blanket. The player whose color came up the most would get points.[3]

The Lenape led a fairly peaceful existence, hunting, growing crops, playing games, building, worshiping, and raising their children to carry on their traditions. Then they got some unexpected and uninvited guests, and their way of life changed forever.

Pahsahëman

How to Play *Pahsahëman*

Two goals, about six feet wide, were staked out on the field about 150 feet long by 60 feet wide. The Lenape used a ball called a *Pahsahikàn*, shaped kind of like a football. It was made of deerskin and stuffed with deer hair. The men could only use their feet to kick the ball toward the goal, while the women could use their hands and feet. Women could tackle while the men could not. The score was kept with a dozen small sticks. Whenever someone would get a point, a stick was taken from the pile and stuck in the ground. When twelve sticks were standing up, whichever team had the most sticks in the ground was the winner.[4]

About Mesingw

A man dressed as Mesingw

One of the important guardian spirits to the Lenape was Mesingw, god of the animals that were hunted by the tribe. Hunters reported seeing Mesingw riding on the back of a deer running through the woods. It was believed he was responsible for the success or failure of a hunt. During ceremonies in the villages, a man would dress as Mesingw, cover himself with a bear skin, and paint his face half red and half black, "talking" to the crowd with a rattle made from a turtle's shell. The ritual was a way to ensure luck for the hunt. Mesingw was also pretty frightening. Parents used the threat of a visit from Mesingw to scare children into behaving.[5]

In 1524, Italian explorer Giovanni da Verrazzano sailed into what is known today as Lower New York Bay.

CHAPTER 4
UNINVITED
GUESTS

The first documented contact between the Lenape and the Europeans happened in 1524.[1] The Italian explorer Giovanni da Verrazzano entered what is known today as Lower New York Bay where he was met by members of the tribe who had rowed out to his ship, the *Dauphine*.

More and more settlers followed Verrazzano. While the English and French primarily settled in New England, the Dutch and Swedish established outposts in *Lenapehoking*. The Dutch settlers and the Lenape began to trade in the furs that were greatly in demand back in Europe. The Lenape also produced the prized wampum, ornate beads made from shells that were used as a kind of money until the Revolutionary War. In return for furs and wampum, the Lenape received from the Europeans new technology such as metal tools, which helped improve their farming and hunting.

This valuable trade created wars among the various tribes, who wanted to dominate trade with the Europeans. The Lenape had battled the Susquehannock Indians in the past, but as trade with the Europeans increased, so did their battles. By 1635, the Susquehannock had pushed the Lenape, who were also suffering from an outbreak of smallpox, from

The Dutch and Swedish established outposts in *Lenapehoking*. They trade for the furs that were in great demand in Europe.

southern Pennsylvania.[2] The Susquehannock themselves were conquered by disease and by the Iroquois. The Lenape were finally able to return to their lands in the 1660s, but by then they were a diminished and weakened people. The Lenape had become part of a "covenant chain," answering to the dominant Iroquois.[3]

The English wrested control of the Lenape homeland from the Dutch in 1664. In 1682, Englishman William Penn, who was a converted Quaker, sought to establish a colony in the New World. He wanted a place where he and his followers could escape persecution and live together in a spirit of brotherly love. As payment for a debt owed to his father, William Penn received a charter from King Charles II of England granting him the lands

William Penn

now called Pennsylvania. The one small problem was that this was the land where the Lenape lived.

As a pacifist, Penn wanted to avoid any kind of violence with the Lenape. In order to get the land his people needed for his colony, he reached out to the Lenape, promising a peaceful coexistence and fair treatment. He and his agents started to purchase the lands from various Lenape chiefs at a price that was fair to both sides. He is believed to have signed a "Great Treaty"

at Shackamaxon not far from Philadelphia. The location for the signing of the treaty had long been a neutral place where the tribes gathered to meet. There they would smoke peace pipes and forge treaties and bonds to keep the peace.[4]

William Penn met with Chief Tamanend and other Lenape chiefs to sign the peace treaty, saying, "We

Statue of Chief Tamanend

Penn made a treaty with Chief Tamanend and the Lenape.

meet on the broad pathway of good faith and good-will; no advantage shall be taken on either side, but all shall be openness and love. We are the same as if one man's body was to be divided into two parts; we are of one flesh and one blood."

Chief Tamanend replied, "We will live in love with William Penn and his children as long as the creeks and rivers run, and while the sun, moon, and stars endure."[5]

And so it was . . . for a while. As with just about any treaty signed between colonists and native inhabitants, the Europeans eventually ignored it. The Lenape's "Great Treaty" with William Penn was no exception.

The Walking Purchase

William Penn's sons John and Thomas did not share their father's belief that the Lenape should be treated fairly. In an attempt to gain more land from the Lenape, a 1686 "lost deed" was shown to the Lenape in 1737. It said the colony had been sold a tract of Lenape land as big as one man could walk in a day and a half. A map was shown to the four Lenape chiefs, who agreed to honor this "deed," but the map was not accurate and misled the chiefs about how much land would be taken.

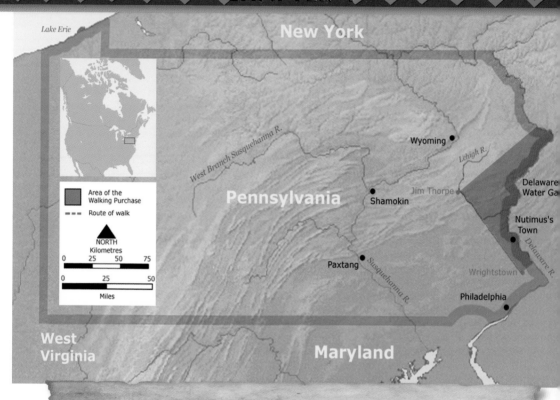

Lake Erie

New York

Area of the
Walking Purchase

Route of walk

NORTH
Kilometres
0   25   50   75

0   25   50
Miles

West
Virginia

Pennsylvania

West Branch Susquehanna R.

Wyoming

Lehigh R.

Jim Thorpe

Delaware
Water Ga

Shamokin

Nutimus's
Town

Paxtang

Susquehanna R.

Wrightstown

Delaware R.

Philadelphia

Maryland

This map shows the 1,200 square mile of land lost by Lenape in eastern Pennsylvania following the Walking Purchase of 1737.

Thomas Penn hired the fastest "walkers" he could find to mark the distance, which began at the fork of the Delaware and Lehigh Rivers. When the "walkers" were finished a day and a half later (after zipping through a path made clear ahead of time), the Lenape had lost about 1,200 square miles of their land. Despite their protests at having been swindled, they were forced to move.[6]

The Story of Penelope Stout

In 1642, a young Dutch woman named Penelope married a man named Kent van Princis and they decided to start a new life in the New World. However, as they traveled across the Atlantic Ocean, a storm struck their ship as it neared what is today Sandy Hook, New Jersey. Penelope and her sick husband were some of the few to escape drowning when the ship was destroyed on the rocks.

Penelope Stout commemorative coin

After the couple swam to shore, Kent was too sick to travel any farther. Their fellow survivors feared Indian attacks and abandoned the pair to their fate. Penelope and her husband hid in a hollow tree, but they were found and attacked by two natives. Kent was killed immediately and Penelope was severely injured and left for dead. She was discovered, as the story goes, by an old Lenape man from the village of Chaquasit.

The Lenape man took her to the village, where she was nursed back to health. She was eventually freed when a ransom was paid for all settlers captured during recent battles between the natives and the settlers. She and the old Lenape man remained friends for the rest of their lives.

Upon her return to New Amsterdam, she met and married a man named Richard Stout. They bought land from the Lenape at Chaquasit and started a settlement called Middletown. It is said that in 1650, her Lenape friends from the village warned her of an impending attack by the sachem Oratam. Penelope and her family were able to survive. She lived, it is said, to be 110 years old, having given birth to ten children.[7]

During the Seven Years' War between the French and the British, thirteen tribal nations, including the Lenape and the Iroquois, fought alongside the French. For this reason, the conflict is also known as the French and Indian War.

CHAPTER 5
LOSING
LENAPEHOKING

From the early 1600s to the late 1700s, the sachem of the Lenape and other nearby tribes signed hundreds of deeds that basically ended their sovereignty of the Lenape homeland. It is not as if they wanted to give up their land, but the sheer volume of settlers flowing into the country—along with the devastation to the Lenape population from the diseases and wars—made holding on to it impossible. At the time of William Penn's arrival, the population of surviving Lenape was estimated to be about 4,000 people. That is about one-fifth of the pre-colonial population.

The Lenape, as with other Native American tribes, did not consider land to be a thing that could be bought or sold. They believed that the money the colonists gave them was more like a gift in exchange for shared use of the land, not an outright purchase. Native Americans also did not understand the "legal" result of signing a paper by putting a mark next to your name.

Over and over, treaties were made and broken, wars were fought and lost, and the Lenape were pushed farther and farther west by repeated removals. During the Seven Years' War (1756–1763), thirteen tribal nations, including the Lenape

Lenape-Delaware Forced Migration

As settlers from Europe flooded their lands, the tribes of the Lenape were pushed farther and farther west.

and the Iroquois, signed the 1758 Treaty of Easton with the British at a meeting in Easton, Pennsylvania. The treaty ended the tribes' alliance with the French and effectively gave away the Lenape's traditional lands. In return, the Native Americans were promised that the land beyond the Allegheny Mountains would be theirs, safe from further encroachment by European settlers. The British ignored the treaty almost immediately.

Over the next century, the Lenape were pushed farther west and up into Canada. In 1867, the U.S. government forced the main group, despite the pleas of the tribe, to relocate from their homes in Kansas to Oklahoma where they were to join the Cherokee Nation in Indian Territory.

Lenape Story: Hunter and Eagle

The Lenape thought a hunter to be both brave and blessed with good fortune if he could pull a tail feather from a live eagle. Because of this, many young hunters wanted to capture one to wear. One young hunter was very rash and greedy. He was determined to get the best feathers. He brought bait he knew the eagles liked to eat to the hills where they lived. He placed the bait on a rock then hid, hoping to trap an eagle by using a forked stick. An eagle came to take the bait, but the hunter thought it too small and chased it away. More eagles came, but he decided they were also too small or their feathers did not look perfect.

The hunter viewed the eagles and judged them too small.

Suddenly, a giant eagle with blood-red feathers came out of the sky. It snatched up the young hunter in its claws and carried him to the top of a mountain. The giant eagle dropped the hunter into a nest with four baby eagles. It said, "You will stay here and watch these young eagles until they have grown to be big enough to carry you. Then they will return you to where I found you. I am the chief of all eagles. You were displeased with the feathers I offered. Now you will suffer here because of your greed. Perhaps when you return from this trial you will be happy with the feathers you are given." The chief of eagles flew away, leaving the young man to care for the babies.

The hunter cared for them very well and they came to love him. The chief of eagles brought deer or rabbit for them to eat. After many, many days, the young eagles learned to fly. They left the hunter in the nest, lonely and worried they would not return.

One day, the chief of eagles flew to the nest and said, "My children will return you to where I found you and I will follow to make sure this

happens safely." Two of the young eagles picked up the hunter, and they flew from the mountaintop down to the forest. There, the man found several eagle feathers, which he collected and carried back to his village, happy and satisfied with the gift he had received.[1]

It is estimated that about 20,000 Lenape, or Delaware Indians, live in North America. About half live in Oklahoma, where the United States officially recognizes two original Lenape tribes: The Delaware Tribe of Western Oklahoma, located in Anadarko, and the Delaware Tribe of Indians based in Bartlesville.[2]

Other tribes of Lenape, such as those located in Pennsylvania, Wisconsin, Ontario, and New Jersey, continue to practice and embrace their heritage, but they do not have reservations and are not officially federally recognized.

Many Lenape traditions, such as certain songs and dances or crafting skills, were lost to the passage of time and to the tribal relocations. But the Lenape tribe of today strives to keep their culture alive for future generations. They still play *Pahsahëman* and hold Stomp Dances. Language classes are available for those who want to learn how their ancestors spoke. Some of these words are on the next page. As you say them, think about the lives of the Lenape people long ago, when they shared the land with the animals, the forests, the lakes and rivers, and their fellow Native Americans.

Lenape Vocabulary[3]

hello	*hè**	red	*màxke*
boy	*pilaechëch*	blue	*aone*
girl	*xkwechëch*	black	*sëke*
man	*lënu*	white	*wòpe*
woman	*xkwe*		
house	*wikëwam*	one	*kwëti*
river	*sipu*	two	*nisha*
lake	*mënëpèkw*	three	*naxa*
water	*mpi*	four	*newa*
trees	*hìtkuk*	five	*palenàxk*
sky	*mushhàkw*	six	*kwëtash*
sun	*kioux*	seven	*nishash*
dog	*mwekane*	eight	*xash*
bear	*màxkw*	nine	*pèshkunk*
deer	*ayape*	ten	*tèlën*

*The Lenape words are pronounced as they are spelled.

1. Women were very respected in Lenape society and were considered equally important as the men within the tribe.

2. Neighboring tribes called the Lenape "the Grandfathers" out of respect for their ability to negotiate peace between tribes in conflict.[1]

3. The Lenape were divided into three family groups: the Wolf, the Turtle, and the Turkey.

4. The Lenape family groups were matrilineal, meaning they were passed down on the mother's side of the family. If your mother was of the Turkey clan, then you were a Turkey, too. When you grew up, you could not marry a Turkey; you had to marry someone from the Wolf or Turtle clan.

5. The three main crops of the Lenape—beans, squash, and corn—were called the Three Sisters.

6. The Lenape did not have horses. They sometimes used dogs as beasts of burden.

7. The Lenape believed that guardian spirits, called *manetuwak,* inhabited everything in nature, from animals to trees to the weather. These spirits were to be respected and honored.

8. The Lenape held a twelve-day annual harvest ceremony in autumn called the *Gamwing,* or Big House Ceremony. Visions were recounted, dances performed, and songs were sung to give thanks for the blessings of the year past and to seek good fortune in the year to come.

9. Every spring, the Lenape played a ball game called *Pahsahëman* that pitted men against women. It was like football and soccer rolled into one. Men could only use their feet, but women could grab the ball with their hands and tackle other players.

10. By 2015, about 20,000 Lenape lived in North America. About half of these were in Oklahoma, where the United States officially recognizes two original Lenape tribes.[2]

Introduction

1. "The Lenape Creation Story," *The Lenape Nation,* March 2015, http://www. lenapenation.org/Lenape Lixsewakan Achimawakana/The Lenape Creation Story.pdf

Chapter One

1. *Delaware Tribe of Indians,* March 2015, http://delawaretribe.org/blog/2013/06/26/faqs/
2. Daniel G. Brinton, *The Lenape and Their Legends* (Philadelphia: D.G. Brinton, 1885), p. 36.
3. *Lenape Lifeways,* March 2015, http://www. lenapelifeways.org/lenape1.htm
4. Richard C. Adams, *Legends of the Delaware Indians and Picture Writing* (Washington, D.C.: 1905; Syracuse, NY: Syracuse University Press, 1997), p. 28.

Chapter Two

1. *Lenape Lifeways,* March 2015, http://www. lenapelifeways.org/lenape2.htm
2. Ibid.
3. *Delaware Tribe of Indians,* April 2015, http://delawaretribe.org/blog/2013/06/27/lenape-canoes/
4. Alan E. Carman, *Footprints in Time: A History and Ethnology of the Lenape-Delaware Indian Culture* (Bloomington, IN: Trafford Publishing, 2013), Kindle file 2169.
5. Carman, Kindle file 2295.

Chapter Three

1. *Lenape Lifeways,* March 2015, http://www. lenapelifeways.org/lenape3.htm#beliefs
2. *Lenape Lifeways.*
3. *Delaware Tribe of Indians,* March 2015, http://delawaretribe.org/blog/2013/06/26/faqs/
4. *Delaware Tribe of Indians,* March 2015, http://delawaretribe.org/blog/2013/06/27/pahsahman-the-lenape-indian-football-game/
5. *Lenape Lifeways.*

Chapter Four

1. Carman, Kindle file 3206
2. *Penn Treaty Museum,* April 2015, http://www.penntreatymuseum.org/americans.php
3. Amy C. Schutt, *Peoples of the River Valleys: The Odyssey of the Delaware Indians* (Philadelphia: University of Pennsylvania Press, 2007). Kindle file 1320.
4. "William Penn's Treaty with the Indians at Shackamaxon," *Penn Treaty Museum,* April 2015, http://penntreatymuseum.org/wordpress/history-2/peace-treaty/
5. Ibid.
6. Steven C. Harper, "The Map That Reveals the Deception of the 1737 Walking Purchase." *The Pennsylvania Magazine of History and Biography* 136.4 (October 2012), pp. 457–460.
7. Alan E. Carman, *Footprints in Time: A History and Ethnology of the Lenape-Delaware Indian Culture* (Bloomington, IN: Trafford Publishing, 2013), Kindle file 3804.

Chapter Five

1. Richard C. Adams, *Legends of the Delaware Indians and Picture Writing* (Washington, D.C.: 1905; Syracuse, NY: Syracuse University Press, 1997), p. 46.
2. Adams, p. xvii.
3. *Lenape Talking Dictionary,* April 2015, http://www.talk-lenape.org.

Ten Fascinating Facts about the Lenape

1. Alan E. Carman, *Footprints in Time: A History and Ethnology of the Lenape-Delaware Indian Culture* (Bloomington, IN: Trafford Publishing, 2013), Kindle file 878.
2. Penn Treaty Museum, "The Population of the Lenni Lenape," http://www. penntreatymuseum.org/americans.php#population

Books

Brown, James W., and Rita T. Kohn. *Long Journey Home: Oral Histories of Contemporary Delaware Indians.* Bloomington: Indiana University Press, 2008.

Bush Gibson, Karen. *Native American History for Kids: With 21 Activities.* Chicago Review Press, 2010.

Donehoo, Dr. George P. *Indian Villages and Place Names in Pennsylvania.* Mechanicsburg, PA: Sunbury Press, 2014.

Vizzi, Greg. *The Original People: The Story of the Lenape Indians by Chief Quiet Thunder and Greg Vizzi.* Nature's Wisdom Press, 2014.

Works Consulted

Adams, Richard C. *Legends of the Delaware Indians and Picture Writing.* Washington, D.C.: 1905; Syracuse, NY: Syracuse University Press, 1997.

Brinton, Daniel G. *The Lenape and Their Legends,* Philadelphia: D.G. Brinton, 1885.

Caffrey, Margaret M. "Complementary Power: Men and Women of the Lenni Lenape." *American Indian Quarterly* 24.1 (Winter 2000): 44–63.

Carman, Alan E. *Footprints in Time: A History and Ethnology of the Lenape-Delaware Indian Culture.* Bloomington, IN: Trafford Publishing, 2013.

Delaware Tribe of Indians. http://delawaretribe.org/

Harper, Steven C. "The Map That Reveals the Deception of the 1737 Walking Purchase." *The Pennsylvania Magazine of History and Biography* 136.4 (October 2012): 457–460.

Lenape Lifeways. www.lenapelifeways.org

Lenape Nation. www.lenapenation.org

Lenape Talking Dictionary. http://www.talk-lenape.org/

Miller, Jay. "Old Religion among the Delawares: The Gamwing (Big House Rite)." *Ethnohistory* 44.1 (Winter 1997): 113–134.

Penn Treaty Museum. www.penntreatymuseum.org

Schutt, Amy C. *Peoples of the River Valleys: The Odyssey of the Delaware Indians.* Philadelphia: University of Pennsylvania Press, 2007.

Soderlund, Jean R. *Delaware Valley Society Before William Penn.* Philadelphia: University of Pennsylvania Press, 2014.

Thompson, Mark L. *The Contest for the Delaware Valley: Allegiance, Identity and Empire in the Seventeenth Century.* Baton Rouge: Louisiana State University Press, 2013.

Treuer, Anton. *Atlas of Indian Nations.* Washington, D.C.: National Geographic, 2013.

On the Internet

Delaware Nation http://www.delawarenation.com/

Delaware Tribe of Indians http://delawaretribe.org/

Museum of Indian Culture, Allentown, PA
http://www.museumofindianculture.org/

Barkhouse—A large, rectangular building built to house several families.

Covenant chain—A series of alliances mainly between the Iroquois and the British that sought to preserve trade and peace.

Gamwing—The annual twelve-day harvest ceremony held in autumn, also called the Big House Ceremony.

Kishelemukong—The Great Spirit who created the universe and everything in it.

Kokolesh—A game using a cone with a rabbit tail on the end tied to a sharp stick. The idea was to catch the cone on the end of the stick.

Lenapehoking—The land where the Lenape lived, a territory that included parts of the modern states of Pennsylvania, New Jersey, Delaware, and Maryland.

Mamandin—A Lenape game played where colored dice made from bones or fruit pits are put in a bowl then dumped onto a blanket.

Manetuwak—Guardian spirits that inhabited everything in nature, from animals to trees to the weather.

Mesingw—An important guardian spirit to the Lenape, god of the animals that were hunted by the tribe.

Munsee—People of the Stony Country, the Lenape who lived north of the Raritan River.

Muxulhemenshi—A tulip tree, one of the trees the Lenape used to make their dugout canoes.

Nanapush—The spirit who is the grandfather of animals and man.

Pahsahëman—A springtime co-ed soccer match pitting males against females.

Pimewakan—A sweat hut that served as a place of worship, a medical tent, and a public bath.

Sachem—The chief chosen for his wisdom and fairness who led each village.

Selahtikàn—A Lenape game using decorated reeds mixed with plain ones and dropped onto a blanket.

Three Sisters—Corn, beans, and squash, the three main crops grown by the Lenape.

Tumpline—A strap used to carry heavy burdens; it was attached to the top of a person's head so that the spine could take some of the weight from the shoulders.

Unalactigo—People by the Ocean, the Lenape who were blended into the Unami by the late 17th century.

Unami—People Down River, the Lenape who lived south of the Raritan River.

Vision Quest—A journey taken by a Lenape teenager in the woods, where he would meet the guardian spirit that would guide and protect him throughout life.

Walking Purchase—A 1737 swindle of the Lenape that cost them 1,200 square miles of their homeland.

Wampum—Ornate beads made from shells that were used as a kind of money until the Revolutionary War.

MEET THE
AUTHOR

Despite being a dashingly handsome, globe-trotting, award-winning photojournalist and travel writer based in New Orleans, Michael DeMocker is, in truth, really quite dull, a terrible dancer, and a frequent source of embarrassment to his wife, son, and three dogs.